Faith Questions
Truth

KYRA DANIELS

DEFINITION

What is Truth, and Why is it Important? 6
How Do We Know Religion is True? 7

TRUTH AND THE TRANSCENDENT

The Correspondence Theory and Christianity 12
God is Truth 14

TRUTH REVEALED

What is the Bible? 18
How Was the Bible Formed? 19
Accusations Against the Bible 21
The Bible as Eyewitness Testimony 24

TRUTH CORRUPTED

The Liar 28
A People Changed 30
False gods 32
The Noetic Effects of Sin 33

CULTURAL MOVEMENTS

Human Reason Has Not Fallen 36
Science is the Way 37
Accepting Many "Truths" 38

TRUTH AND THE CHURCH

Christian Postmodernism 42
Church Hurt 44

TRUTH REDEEMED

Jesus Christ, The Truth 48
Jesus Christ, The True Prophet 50
His Resurrection and Our Faith 52

HOW TO TRUTHFULLY LIVE

Dealing with Doubt 56
Living with Integrity and Honesty 58
Evangelizing in a Truthless Culture 59

What is Truth, and Why is it *Important?*

Truth is something that is rooted in fact and reality. It can also describe something ideal. Whatever is true is a perfect and excellent representation of its kind. For instance, "a true rose" is not only a real one but also one without flaws or blemishes. Finally, truth is exact. The "true measurement" for a window curtain suggests that the measurement was correct. Not too short or too long, the curtain is a proper fit and falls exactly at the base of a window.

Truth is important for all areas of culture. For instance, relationships are built on truthfulness. When we engage in "truthful conversations" with our best friends, nothing is hidden from them because these friends have proven to be trustworthy. Our legal system investigates truth. For example, in a courtroom, a credible witness gives a true testimony so the actual events of a crime can be judged. Truth also impacts science. It is essential to discover knowledge about the natural world and create efforts for advancement. Finally, truth even influences how we see God. If we view God as true, we will trust in Him, follow His law, and seek to know Him in a relationship with Him. But, in our culture, there are many distortions of truth that challenge our view of God and religion. Having a biblical perspective of truth can help us right these distortions. This booklet will walk us through how to counter falsehoods with the gospel of Jesus Christ so that we can be bearers of truth in the world.

TRUTH IS IMPORTANT FOR ALL AREAS OF CULTURE.

How Do We Know *Religion* is True?

There are three main theories of truth, and these theories shape how our society proves religion to be true. The first theory is the pragmatic theory. Proponents of the pragmatic theory claim truth always has practical results, so whatever works for you is true. According to this theory, a religion is true if it is practically beneficial—if it encourages someone to be a good person or helps one manage stress. We see the application of the pragmatic theory when someone joins a mosque for relational benefit. In this way, one may view Islam as true because of its practical results.

Definition

The second theory is the coherence theory. Proponents of the coherence theory believe that truth is logical and fits within an established set of beliefs. According to this theory, religious beliefs are true if they make sense to a person and are the same as what he or she values. We see the coherence theory applied in this way: Someone who likes to volunteer may agree with the justice and outreach mission of a pagan organization. Therefore, he or she might come to believe that the organization's pagan beliefs were true because its ethics fit with what the person already values.

The last theory is the correspondence theory. This theory holds that truth matches reality. For a claim to be true, there must be outside, observable, and independent facts to prove it. The idea that one's car crashed is deemed true or false based on whether or not it actually happened. Unlike the first two theories, the correspondence theory asserts that truth is objective, which means it is not dependent on one's own feelings, experiences, or reason. According to the correspondence theory, a religion is true if it is proven by an actual historical or natural event.

> **THERE ARE THREE MAIN THEORIES OF TRUTH, AND THESE THEORIES SHAPE HOW OUR SOCIETY PROVES RELIGION TO BE TRUE.**

"IF WE VIEW GOD AS TRUE, WE WILL TRUST IN HIM, FOLLOW HIS LAW, AND SEEK TO KNOW HIM IN A RELATIONSHIP WITH HIM."

PART TWO

truth and the transcendent

The Correspondence Theory and Christianity

The pragmatic and coherence theories have limits. They only provide personal evidence for a religious belief, so such belief cannot be universally true. But the correspondence theory is the strongest theory for deciding whether or not a religion is true without exception because it provides independent and objective evidence for its claims based on the historical or natural events that support it.

Christianity is based on the correspondence theory. Its truth claims are the result of God's independent activity in the world and His revelation to us. Central to Christianity, the gospel is the claim that

Jesus Christ is the eternal Son who, with God the Father and God the Holy Spirit, formed a plan to save His people from sin, and sin is disobedience against God's law. God the Son descended from His heavenly throne and took on flesh. Jesus lived a perfect life and was completely obedient to the Father. He was punished and died on the cross to pay for our sins. His body lay in the tomb, but on the third day, He rose from the grave in glory and honor. Because of His obedience, He conquered sin and death, and the Father exalted Him. Jesus ascended to the right hand of God, where He reigns now. Through our faith in Christ, believers receive the gift of eternal life in the presence of God. The saving work of Jesus is the gospel. It is true, not because of personal benefit or logic but because the events of Jesus's ministry actually happened, and historical evidence further proves what we already know to be true about biblical events.

> CENTRAL TO CHRISTIANITY, THE GOSPEL IS THE CLAIM THAT JESUS CHRIST IS THE ETERNAL SON WHO, WITH GOD THE FATHER AND GOD THE HOLY SPIRIT, FORMED A PLAN TO SAVE HIS PEOPLE FROM SIN, AND SIN IS DISOBEDIENCE AGAINST GOD'S LAW.

God is Truth

Evidence for Christianity is found in the world but starts with the person of Christ. Christianity argues that truth comes from God revealing His transcendence, which is His extraordinary essence beyond the physical world. Scripture claims that when we look at the beauty of nature and the complexity of human design, we have an understanding that there must be an intelligent, spiritual being who has created all. Romans 1:19-20 states that "what can be known about God is evident among them, because God has shown it to them. For his invisible attributes, that is, his eternal power and divine nature, have been clearly seen since the creation of the world, being understood through what he has made." This knowledge of God's infinite nature is called "general revelation." While we cannot know everything about God, His unmatched majesty, power, and creativity are on display when we look at the ocean and see the sunrise. We discover God's holiness, which describes how His being, reason, and abilities are perfect and different from us. In His holiness, God stands with ultimate authority and superiority over us. He is the infinite Creator, and humans are His finite creatures. God created our reality, and truth is based on what He has willed and established. Therefore, our understanding of what is true must be revealed by Him.

For God to be the originator of truth, God must be truth Himself. The fullness of what is true rests in God. He is ultimate and excellent, without flaw or error. God is truthful in speech, character, and action (Exodus 34:6). Numbers 23:19 states, "God is not a man, that he might lie, or a son of man, that he might change his mind. Does he speak and not act, or promise and not fulfill?" Faithful and trustworthy, God will never change. He is the true God; there is no other like Him. His will and ways are righteous and just, doing no wrong and bearing no lie. The true God has defined truth, so we should seek Him for revelation. He will lead us to proper worship and true religion. When all other theories and religions fail, His Word will remain and give us enduring evidence for our belief in Him.

> FOR GOD TO BE THE ORIGINATOR OF TRUTH, GOD MUST BE TRUTH HIMSELF. THE FULLNESS OF WHAT IS TRUE RESTS IN GOD.

PART THREE

truth
revealed

What is *the Bible?*

God has revealed truth through the Bible, which is His written Word to us. In the last section, we explained "general revelation" as the knowledge of God's transcendent presence, creative power, and unmatched divine authority conveyed through the natural world. God graciously revealed this truth to us, and therefore, we all have the understanding that He is worthy of our adoration and the obligation to worship Him. But, to redeem us from sin, remove our guilt, and enable us to worship Him, God continued to speak through special revelation.

Special revelation is the truth of God's plan of salvation revealed in Scripture. This revelation points to the person and saving work of Jesus Christ. Because it is God's own product, Scripture reflects the nature of its author. For example, because God is true, the Bible is also true. It is without error or imperfection. Scripture is also trustworthy. We can rely on it to guide us on the right path in life and give us solid ground in a world of conflicting worldviews. The Bible is authoritative. When we come to Scripture, we are reading instructions from the Lord of the universe. Every part is important to apply to our hearts so that we are convicted of sin and grow in spiritual maturity. The Bible is eternal. Though time passes, God's Word is unchanging. Isaiah 40:8 says, "The grass withers, the flowers fade, but the word of our God remains forever." The wisdom of Scripture remains true and relevant for each generation and culture. Finally, the Bible is sufficient. Since Scripture is the very Word of God, whose reality is independent and objective, it does not make sense to seek any other resource. God, the ultimate source of truth, has spoken, and His Word communicates all that we need to know about the world, ourselves, salvation, and our future hope in Christ.

How was the Bible *Formed?*

The Bible was inspired by the Holy Spirit through the use of human authors. We read in 2 Peter 1:21 that "no prophecy ever came by the will of man; instead, men spoke from God as they were carried along by the Holy Spirit." God was the true author but spoke through ordinary men under the guidance of the Holy Spirit. These men were not in a trance but indeed had intellectual awareness, physical ability, and knowledge through the power of God as they were writing. God used nearly forty authors over 1500 years through multiple literary genres, such as historical narrative, prophecy, law, and poetry. The Bible was originally written in three languages, which were Hebrew, Aramaic, and

Koine Greek, and includes 66 individual books. Through the diversity of Scripture, there is also harmony. The Bible is one unified story of God working in history to accomplish His plan of redemption through Jesus Christ. Scripture records the spoken words of God, His activity, and the lived experiences of people who encountered the Lord.

The Bible consists of two parts: the Old Testament and New Testament. The Old Testament is the divine text for both Jews and Christians. With its first book, Genesis, written as early as the 15th century BCE, the Old Testament traces the historical narrative of the ancient Israelites. The Israelites were God's chosen people through whom He revealed His plan of redemption. Their lives pointed to the need for a Savior, and throughout the Old Testament, God revealed symbols to show how His saving work would be accomplished. With its last book, Revelation, written as late as 95 AD, the New Testament records the life, death, resurrection, and rule of Jesus Christ, the promised Savior. The New Testament authors and Jesus Himself cited specific prophecies to prove the Son of God had come to reveal the fullness of truth from the signs in the Old Testament. The New Testament also includes how the gospel spread and how the early Church was formed as a result.

The formation of Scripture can be an issue for Christians who struggle in their faith. We might wonder how an ancient text with so many voices, genres, and time periods could communicate the one voice of God and be relevant for today. But, if we seek out God's revelation, if we commit to studying the Bible regularly, God will bring unity from the diversity. He will connect the dots for us so that the gospel of Jesus Christ is abundantly clear from the beginning of the Bible to the end. Though He is transcendent, God is also immanent, which means He has control over the details of life. God will show how He knit history, genres, people, and languages together for His good purposes. The diversity of Scripture does not have to be something that turns us away, but it can lead us to marvel at the truth of God.

Accusations Against *the Bible*

Opponents of Christianity make two claims against Scripture. Both claims accuse Scripture of being false, and therefore, deny that the gospel of Jesus Christ is true. But let us remember that what is true can usually be proven by real evidence in the world. We can use this evidence to support the historical accuracy of Scripture and counter false accusations.

Those in opposition to Christianity claim that the story of Scripture was imagined and historically unreliable. They argue that the Bible is full of mythological stories created by ancient people. But we can utilize evidence from archaeological findings and unbiased historical documents. For instance, the narrative and prophecy of the Old Testament tell of and predict the rise of the kingdom of Israel, its downfall to the Babylonian Empire, the exile, and the rebuilding of Jerusalem. Ancient war logs, clay tablets, and royal inscriptions of kings discovered from that biblical era prove these accounts to be true. Additionally, even non-Christian historians of the ancient past verified the accounts depicted in the New Testament. In his history of the Roman Empire, an ancient Roman pagan named Cornelius Tacitus corroborated Jesus's death sentence under Pontius Pilate. He also wrote about the torture that early Christians encountered as a result of their faith. Another famous, ancient historian named Flavius Josephus was a Jewish man who did not believe that Jesus was the Son of God. But, in his major historical work, Josephus cited that the disciples did claim that Jesus was the promised Savior and saw His risen body. Events in the Bible were mirrored in the world, so Scripture serves as a historically accurate document.

The second claim against Christianity is that the Bible was changed from its original version. As a result, opponents of the faith argue that the message or intent of the authors was lost over the years. In response, we can explain how, similar to the Old Testament, the documentation of the New Testament has been handed down in a consistent and traceable way. Biblical scholars argue that we can know that the gospel account of Jesus is the original and unaltered claim of Christianity because archaeologists have discovered over 5800 distinct yet agreeing, handwritten copies of the Greek New Testament. This number is more than that of any other ancient text. Textual critics have compared the documents and identified few changes, and these changes consisted of minor spelling errors rather than major contradictions in doctrine. By God's grace, the ancient scribes wrote about the gospel of Jesus Christ over 5800 times because they knew it was the truth for a weary world and sought to preserve its message from error.

BY GOD'S GRACE, THE ANCIENT SCRIBES WROTE ABOUT THE GOSPEL OF JESUS CHRIST OVER 5800 TIMES BECAUSE THEY KNEW IT WAS THE TRUTH FOR A WEARY WORLD AND SOUGHT TO PRESERVE ITS MESSAGE FROM ERROR.

"LET US REMEMBER THAT WHAT IS TRUE CAN USUALLY BE PROVEN BY REAL EVIDENCE IN THE WORLD. WE CAN USE THIS EVIDENCE TO SUPPORT THE HISTORICAL ACCURACY OF SCRIPTURE AND COUNTER FALSE ACCUSATIONS."

The Bible as
Eyewitness Testimony

The fact that Jesus's life, death, and resurrection were seen by many is evidence that they are true. Scripture records eyewitness testimonies. The gospel accounts were written about forty to sixty years after Jesus's death, and Paul's letters were written even sooner. Because of such early New Testament documentation, the original eyewitnesses were still around and served as primary sources of information. Luke 1:1-4 states, "Many have undertaken to compile a narrative about the events that have been fulfilled among us, just as the original eyewitnesses and servants of the word handed them down to us. It also seemed good to me, since I have carefully investigated everything from the very first, to write to you in an orderly sequence, most honorable Theophilus, so that you may know the certainty of the things about which you have been instructed." Scripture verifies itself of its authenticity and integrity through the careful record of chosen authors. We can believe that by His sustaining hand, God did not allow any human error or deception to falsify His Word.

Who were the eyewitnesses? They were the poor, the oppressed, and the rejected people of society, like the Samaritan woman in John 4 and the blind man in John 9. If the biblical authors wanted to devise a made-up story about the God-Man to gain power and prestige, they would have used eyewitnesses whom that culture considered "credible." These might have included the religious elite, the wealthy, and the powerful. Rather, we see in the gospels that Jesus confronted these individuals of their wickedness and cared for the humble who trusted in Him. Jesus was not depicted as a great and mighty hero to attract followers and spread an ideology. Instead, He was a ridiculed, meek, and lowly servant who suffered and died to redeem us from sin. Later, His disciples too suffered and died when they spread the good news of Jesus. Even the most committed liar would not sacrifice his life for a false story. But the disciples accepted death and held onto the truth of the gospel until the end.

The testimonies in Scripture show us the boldness of gospel truth. By the Holy Spirit, the eyewitnesses were courageous and preached the truth of Jesus Christ in the face of prejudice and execution. Their conviction helps us see that the gospel must be true and worth telling. Their perseverance inspires us to hold onto God's truth through hardship.

> THE TESTIMONIES IN SCRIPTURE SHOW US HOW BOLD THE GOSPEL TRUTH IS.

The *Liar*

If the Word of God is true, why has the world rejected it? As we see in Genesis 1 and 2, in the beginning, God made creation to reflect His truth. Adam and Eve, the first humans, were honest, transparent, and innocent.

Though creation lived harmoniously in the garden of Eden, spiritual evil was present. Satan, the liar, disguised himself as a serpent. Satan went to Eve and asked her, "Did God really say, 'You can't eat from any tree in the garden'?" (Genesis 3:1). God had commanded Adam not to eat the fruit from only one tree, the Tree of Knowledge of Good and Evil, or else they would die. But Satan confused truth with a lie and implied that God had limited them. Satan then denied the punishment of death for disobeying the Lord's law. He claimed they would instead be like God, knowing good and evil. Satan accused God of being a liar, and Eve fell for his deception.

Like Eve, we too can often see God and His good and wise Word and instruction as untrustworthy. We redefine reality based on the lies of the foolish snake. Some listen to the voices of celebrities, horoscopes, news sources, and peers instead of trusting God's voice. Instead of answering these voices with the truth of God, we question and assume God is withholding something from us. We question ourselves, asking, "Am I *really* a sinner? Do I *really* need a Savior? Does God *really* have my best interest in mind? What am I missing if I follow God?" But through faith in Jesus Christ, we can pray to prioritize the Word of the Lord above all else. When the voice of the liar rings in our ears in an attempt to deceive us, the Holy Spirit will help us answer him with truth and expose his darkness with the light of Scripture.

"BUT THROUGH FAITH IN JESUS CHRIST, WE CAN PRAY TO PRIORITIZE THE WORD OF THE LORD ABOVE ALL ELSE."

A People *Changed*

Adam's and Eve's sin had relational consequences. They became the lie they believed. The first way we see the effect of the lie was in their hiding from each other. At first, Adam and Eve were "naked, yet felt no shame" (Genesis 2:25), symbolizing their openness and transparency. But after sinning, they saw their bodies as something to hide. This reaction showed how their relationship itself would consist of secrecy and suppression of truth. Adam and Eve tried to hide from God as well. Believing the lie not only brought sin and shame but also brought fear. The peace they felt from trusting in the truth of God was gone, and now, they were afraid of their Lord. When God confronted them, they each blamed the other and denied their wrongdoing.

Adam and Eve were removed from the garden of Eden. They were separated from the life-giving presence of Truth Himself and faced death. Inherited from our first parents, we too experience the same relational consequences of sin. Ashamed, we hide from those with whom we should be the closest. We keep secrets, harming the intimacy of marriages and friendships. We even put lies on others when we blame, spread rumors, or falsify someone's character. Most of all, our relationship with God is affected. Rejecting His truth alienates us from God and leads to fear and anxiety. Sin makes us worried, guilty creatures deserving just punishment. But praise be to God that Jesus Christ covers us with His righteousness.

The Savior has restored what we distorted and reconciled us back to God. We do not have to fear punishment, for Jesus took it all on the cross. Whenever we stumble, we can approach God like adopted sons and daughters and rest in His presence. Jesus has also reconciled us to each other. He gives us a new identity in Him and frees us from shame. In Him, we find the confidence to be truthful, regardless of others' opinions. Our relationships will thrive in the newness of life Jesus gives.

> THE SAVIOR HAS RESTORED WHAT WE DISTORTED AND RECONCILED US BACK TO GOD.

False gods

Biblical history highlights how lying drew humanity away from God and toward idolatry. Idolatry is the adoration and reverence of people and things not meant to satisfy. Adam and Eve idolized themselves when they ate from the Tree of Knowledge of Good and Evil. Instead of worshiping God, they worshiped themselves and sought to obtain glory for their own namesake. As the population grew after the fall, people engaged more and more in idolatry. Romans 1:21-23 states, "For though they knew God, they did not glorify him as God or show gratitude. Instead, their thinking became worthless, and their senseless hearts were darkened. Claiming to be wise, they became fools and exchanged the glory of the immortal God for images resembling mortal man, birds, four-footed animals, and reptiles." Humans rejected God's general revelation and acted on what they believed to be true. They created their own statues of brass and metal to worship. They looked at things in nature and made idols out of them. Even God's chosen people, whom He promised to bless and through whom He would redeem the world, fell to idolatry. In Exodus 32:1-4, the Israelites made a calf idol from their golden jewelry and gave the idol credit for saving them from Egyptian slavery. But it was actually God who had protected them, defeated their enemies, and led them out of Egypt. Not only was the golden calf a false god, but the Israelites' worship of it was based on a lie.

How do we worship false gods now? We often believe the lie that things will satisfy us. Our hearts pursue money for stability, career moves for significance, material possessions for identity, and pleasures for meaning. We make these things false gods and let them rule over our lives. In turn, we lie by attributing to them a level of goodness that only belongs to God. But, through our faith in Jesus, the Holy Spirit works in us to center our hearts on true worship. Through Him, we can rid our lives of the idols that would lead us to destruction and instead pursue the grace of God.

The Noetic Effects *of Sin*

Biblical history also depicts how sin corrupted human thinking. This damage to the mind is called the "noetic effects of sin." Romans 1:28 states, "And because they did not think it worthwhile to acknowledge God, God delivered them over to a corrupt mind so that they do what is not right." Our turning away from God and the light of His truth has darkened our cognitive abilities. The noetic effects of sin were seen in the false prophets in Scripture. In the book of Ezekiel, we learn that the continued disobedience of the Israelites led to a fallen kingdom.

The Babylonians attacked the Israelites and exiled some of the people. While in Babylon, God appointed a man named Ezekiel to be a prophet. A prophet spoke God's truth of repentance, coming judgment, and restoration. Ezekiel warned that if the Israelites did not turn from their idolatry, there would be another attack on those left in their homeland, and their temple city, Jerusalem, would be destroyed. But the Israelites, in their distorted reasoning, continued to reject God's word and listened to false prophets. These false prophets spoke lies to the Israelites and claimed they did not have to worry about repentance or God's judgment.

In Ezekiel 13, God told Ezekiel to confront the false prophets who "prophesy out of their own imagination" (Ezekiel 13:2). Like the serpent in the garden of Eden, the false prophets deceived the Israelites and led them to their downfall. The noetic effects of sin still impact us. Apart from God, our thoughts are faulty. We are prone to forget His character and salvation. We need the Holy Spirit to constantly remind us of the gospel and God's eternal truths. We also often believe and perpetuate the wrong things. For example, if we look back on a time when we did not know the gospel or true biblical interpretation, we can see how we might have supported and promoted incorrect beliefs of the culture or misinterpretations of Scripture. We need God to overcome our fallen minds and discern what is true.

PART FIVE

false truths of cultural movements

Human Reason Has Not Fallen

Sin's corruption of truth has not only affected us personally but has also impacted culture. To confront the false worldviews of today, we should study the progression of such corruption throughout history. We can begin with a period called the Age of Enlightenment. During that time, rationalism was valued over religion. Skeptics argued that human reasoning was not damaged by sin—that an individual could look within and use his or her own mental capabilities to discover truth. As a result, knowledge came from the human mind instead of the Word of God. Though skeptics claimed the reality of objective truth, they were mistaken in trusting in human reason alone to obtain it. The human mind is unique and complex. No other of God's creatures has the mental capacity to invent, solve complex problems, and imagine other possibilities for the world. Because we are made in the image of God, humans do have incredible gifts of reason and intellect. However, as stated earlier, sin has distorted the mind, and we must trust in God for understanding. Only He can save us from taking pride in our gifts of reason and intellect and graciously redeem them to be instruments for His glory.

> SIN HAS DISTORTED THE MIND, AND WE MUST TRUST IN GOD FOR UNDERSTANDING.

Science is the Way

The next cultural movement was the emergence of science. The realm of science exploded under the idea that human reason was capable of understanding objective truth. Scientists used the scientific method and observation to discover patterns in the world, test them, and form theories. The era of scientific discovery led to a growing distrust in religion. These skeptics claimed that we could only know what is true through what we can test and observe. They argued we could not know morality, values, and religious beliefs. Science and faith began to duel on the topic of creation and in discussions on the existence of God.

Science is a God-given tool to understand the natural laws and the beautiful world He designed. We can use science to progress society and promote public safety. But in the name of science, skeptics have forsaken the truth of the intelligent Creator who expresses His existence through His creation. Furthermore, skeptics have used science to cast doubt on the spiritual truth that Scripture illuminates. The Bible was not meant to be a detailed scientific textbook. Rather, Scripture is the revelation of the almighty God who created and redeemed the world. He saved us from our moral shortcomings through Jesus's saving works and, in Christ, has enabled us to live in a way that reflects a love for Him and others. This revelation is a truth that science cannot teach us.

Accepting Many "Truths"

After the age of scientific discovery, postmodernism took shape in culture. Postmodernism says that truth is based on experience and is relative. "Relative" means that each culture has formed its own way of looking at things. Each has its own language, philosophy, and social norms to interpret and navigate the world. For instance, in some cultures, it is acceptable to spend an extended period socializing after finishing dinner at a restaurant. Other cultures would find staying at your table after you have eaten inconsiderate to customers waiting for a seat. To postmodernists, truth is even individual. Whatever works best for you or whatever identifies with your personal values is your "truth." Postmodernists apply this idea to religion, so they see all belief systems as true, even when they contradict.

Despite varying cultural norms and personal preferences, there is still the reality of universal truth: God and His will for us through Jesus Christ. We must surrender our individual and cultural values to God and make sure they align with His Word. Christainity is the belief system that is supreme over all. It is not one piece of a puzzle to know God. It is not one path among many viable options. God has provided an exclusive and sure way to reconcile us to Himself. This way was accomplished through the life, death, and resurrection of His Son. Through Scripture, we see how this worldview is not arrogant or for those claiming to be morally superior. Rather, we see it is the product of God's unmerited favor and grace toward rebellious sinners. We discover how God has supplied us who were poor and spiritually deficient with what we need most of all: Him. Out of His love and commitment to us, God has provided the only way to true sustenance and lasting satisfaction.

> THERE IS STILL THE REALITY OF UNIVERSAL TRUTH: GOD AND HIS WILL FOR US THROUGH JESUS CHRIST. WE MUST SURRENDER OUR INDIVIDUAL AND CULTURAL VALUES TO GOD AND MAKE SURE THEY ALIGN WITH HIS WORD.

PART SIX

*truth and
the church*

Christian *Postmodernism*

Truth relativism has challenged the way many Christians look at Scripture interpretation. We live in a society where many worldviews and religions are close to one another. Some believers succumb to the pressures this type of diversity imposes and doubt the absolute truth claims of Christianity. Christian postmodernism assumes that Scripture has been affected by the cultural norms of the people of Israel, so our understanding of Christian beliefs must be altered to obtain a more fitting belief system for our cultural context. For instance, on the subject of LGTBQ+ issues, Christian postmodernists might say that the ancient Israelites saw homosexuality as a sin because of the need to populate their nation at the time. Since such a need to grow the human race is not necessary, postmodernists would argue that our culture does not have the same taboo against homosexuality. Christian postmodernists believe in the saving work of Jesus illuminated in the Bible but do not believe the text is without error. They tend to hold onto the certain aspects of Scripture, like the ethical teachings of Jesus, that agree with modern ideas and reject anything that conflicts. But Christian postmodernists fail to consider that Scripture is the product of Jesus, the true God and Lord of the universe. All of the Bible is truth, spoken out by the triune God—Father, Son, and Holy Spirit. It is certainly important to understand the cultural context of Scripture for proper interpretation, but we can trust that God has given us lasting principles through His commands to the ancient Israelites. When we read the whole of God's Word, we see how the principles expressed through the Israelite culture are fulfilled in the saving work of Jesus Christ and shape how we live as a result. For instance, on the topic of LGBTQ+ issues, in Scripture, we see sexuality is not just a cultural standard for the Israelites, but ultimately, sexuality is a picture of the relationship between Jesus and His Church and the call for us to reflect this truth in marriage.

> CHRISTIAN POSTMODERNISM ASSUMES THAT SCRIPTURE HAS BEEN AFFECTED BY THE CULTURAL NORMS OF THE PEOPLE OF ISRAEL, SO OUR UNDERSTANDING OF CHRISTIAN BELIEFS MUST BE ALTERED TO OBTAIN A MORE FITTING BELIEF SYSTEM FOR OUR CULTURAL CONTEXT.

Church *Hurt*

We must recognize that there are many Christians who doubt the Bible and question the truth of Christianity, not because of the influence of other religions but as a result of spiritual abuse. The historical involvement of Christians in colonization and slavery can unsettle a believer's faith. Additionally, personal injustices in the local church, abuse from a trusted mentor, and the general disappointment felt when a famous pastor is exposed of wrongdoing can leave many to wonder if the gospel is true. How can the saving work of Jesus be true when there are so many Christians who do, say, and believe awful things? Fortunately, God answers this question in His Word. 1 John 4:20 states, "If anyone says, 'I love God,' and yet hates his brother or sister, he is a liar. For the person who does not love his brother or sister whom he has seen cannot love God whom he has not seen." Jesus Himself called the Pharisees, the hypocrites of His day, "whitewashed tombs" (Matthew 23:27) because they focused on clean outward appearances but were corrupt on the inside. Those who are true believers will produce fruit as evidence of how they live their lives. While only the Lord knows people's hearts, a person who shows no signs of a transformed life may not be a true believer. These lives are not marked and changed by the truth of God. Rather, like the serpent in Eden, they deceive.

Even when we are rattled by Christian hypocrisy and spiritual abuse, we can find comfort that God knows the human heart (Psalm 44:21). God will expose all deceit in His time, so we can mourn for an abuser's sin and pray for that person's repentance. God will give us discernment to identify true Christianity—faith that loves God, cares for others more than self, seeks justice, and lives out of humble gratitude for salvation. Let us not look at the Bible and Christianity through the lens of our traumas, but let us give our traumas to the Lord and ask Him to preserve our faith when we are hurt.

"GOD WILL GIVE US DISCERNMENT TO IDENTIFY TRUE CHRISTIANITY—FAITH THAT LOVES GOD, CARES FOR OTHERS MORE THAN SELF, SEEKS JUSTICE, AND LIVES OUT OF HUMBLE GRATITUDE FOR SALVATION."

PART SEVEN

truth redeemed

Jesus Christ, *the Truth*

We have discussed how much sin has impacted truth in biblical history, in the world, and in ourselves. But praise be to God that He has not left us in our sin and false natures. As we mentioned before, God has revealed the way of redemption in human history and, through His written Word, pointed to the person and saving work of Jesus Christ. As God planned in eternity past, the eternal Son of God was sent into the world. God introduced His coming in Genesis 3:15 which states, "I will put hostility between you and the woman, and between your offspring and her offspring. He will strike your head, and you will strike his heel." After Adam and Eve received the punishment for their disobedience, God cursed the serpent. This curse gave Adam and Eve hope. God promised that Eve's offspring, a Savior, would come and defeat the liar, Satan. The Promised Son came in the person of Jesus Christ. He is the Redeemer, and we too can have hope in Him, for His saving work set us free from Satan's grip.

In his gospel account, the disciple John said Jesus was the eternal Word, or *Logos* in Greek (John 1:1). *Logos* was an idea among ancient Greek philosophers that conveyed there was a divine and unchanging truth that regulated the universe. This truth was transcendent yet immanent and knowable. John referred to Jesus as the *Logos*, or eternal Word, to declare His divine authority. One in essence with the Father and Holy Spirit, Jesus was God, the transcendent Creator, and revealed Him fully. And, according to John, Jesus came near; He took on flesh and lived among us. In John 14:6, Jesus declared, "I am the way, the truth, and the life. No one comes to the Father except through me." He brought light to our sin-darkened minds. Because of Jesus, we have been shown divine truth and can come to know Him. This knowledge leads us to salvation and peace with God.

"THE PROMISED SON CAME IN THE PERSON OF JESUS CHRIST. HE IS THE REDEEMER, AND WE TOO CAN HAVE HOPE IN HIM, FOR HIS SAVING WORK SET US FREE FROM SATAN'S GRIP."

Jesus Christ,
the True Prophet

A prophet was a person who proclaimed the will and words of God. Throughout biblical history, we see many prophets who, under the Holy Spirit, spoke of the coming Savior. But Jesus was the true Prophet; He not only spoke the very words of the Lord, but He fulfilled the words of the old prophets (Luke 24:44). The Old Testament was full of prophecies that predicted the work and arrival of the Anointed Son, and the New Testament authors cited these specific prophecies to prove Jesus was who He said He was. As a result, we see that all of Scripture points to Jesus as the Promised One. Isaiah 7:14 predicts the Savior would be born of a virgin; Isaiah 35:5-6 foretells He would perform healing miracles; and Isaiah 53 explains how He would suffer for the payment of sin. As we know from New

Testament, eyewitness documentation, Jesus was born of a virgin (Luke 1:27), healed the sick (Matthew 14:14), and died on the cross to remove our guilt (Matthew 27:32-56).

As the true Prophet, the One who delivered God's Words, Jesus spoke the truth and resisted lies. He demonstrated this faithfulness when He was tested in the wilderness in Matthew 4:1-11. During this time, Satan came to Him. Like he did in the garden of Eden, Satan twisted the Word of God and tried to deceive Jesus into disobeying three times. But Jesus remained obedient to the Lord and spoke truth to counter each of Satan's lies.

Jesus was a prophet like Moses, the man who delivered the Israelites from slavery (Deuteronomy 18:15-19). In His offense against Satan, Jesus repeated Moses's commands, which pronounced truth and loyalty to God above all. But Jesus was also a prophet better than Moses; Jesus always trusted in God's Word and never sinned. In this way, Jesus proved He was the true Prophet. We can trust that Jesus's words are true, authoritative, and final (Hebrews 1:1-2). As the person with the most power, a judge in a courtroom has the last word, and when he or she stops speaking and the judge's gavel falls to announce that court is dismissed, the stenographer stops writing the court document. Like a judge, Jesus has spoken the final word, and thus, His Scripture is complete, trustworthy, and eternal. No one or nothing after Him can replace.

HE NOT ONLY SPOKE THE VERY WORDS OF THE LORD, BUT HE FULFILLED THE WORDS OF THE OLD PROPHETS.

His Resurrection and *Our Faith*

The Bible is a historically accurate document and testimony that proves Jesus's ministry. But Christianity is more than the fact of His existence and work. Christianity is the belief that the person and saving work of Jesus actually affects us. The historical record and testimony of Scripture have a purpose as we see that biblical authors wanted to point to the truth of Jesus and His trustworthiness. Through His miracles, Jesus proved He was the Son of God and, thereby, showed that we can trust in Him as our Savior.

We can believe that Jesus truly did come to give us life and freedom from sin. Jesus verified this commitment through His greatest miracle: His resurrection from the grave. The empty tomb and the hundreds of eyewitnesses who saw His risen body (1 Corinthians 15:3-8) gave proof that Jesus had defeated sin and death. However, this act was not isolated. God meant for Jesus's resurrection to also free us from the power of the grave.

Because of our sin, we received the punishment of death and eternal separation from God. But Jesus's death on our behalf and His powerful resurrection are proof that our sins have been forgiven and eternal life is guaranteed. We did not receive the judgment that we deserved. Now, we can look forward to forever resting in the presence of God. To receive this gift, we must trust, or have faith in, Jesus. Hebrews 11:1 says, "Now faith is the reality of what is hoped for, the proof of what is not seen." Though we have not seen the risen Jesus in this lifetime, we have an assurance of our salvation and the fact that we will meet Him when He returns. Because He truly lives, we have confident hope that God keeps His promises and will raise us into eternal life with Christ. Our faith rests on a solid foundation; it is based on the truth of Jesus's historical victory.

"WE CAN BELIEVE THAT JESUS TRULY DID COME TO GIVE US LIFE AND FREEDOM FROM SIN. JESUS VERIFIED THIS COMMITMENT THROUGH HIS GREATEST MIRACLE: HIS RESURRECTION FROM THE GRAVE."

PART EIGHT

how to truthfully live

Dealing with *Doubt*

Read John 20:24-29 and Luke 24:13-35

In the last section, we talked about faith being the evidence for what is unseen. However, we must admit that we can still struggle with our faith. So many generations removed, we have not seen the risen Jesus and so may find ourselves doubting the truth of the resurrection. But there is comfort in Scripture. God provides biblical examples of doubt and how to deal with it. The disciple Thomas was not with the other disciples when the risen Jesus first appeared among them. When the disciples told Thomas what they saw, Thomas doubted because he had not seen the sight himself. He would not believe unless he saw and touched the marks where

Jesus's hands were nailed to the cross. A week later, Jesus appeared among them again and offered His scarred body for Thomas to see and touch. Jesus did not condemn Thomas for his doubt, for He knew Thomas was a truth seeker. So Jesus provided him the evidence for believing. Underneath our doubt is a desire to know the truth and not be swept away by a false story. We who wrestle with doubt do not have to be discouraged. Like Thomas, we can ask Jesus, who will give us what we need to believe.

Another biblical example of doubt is seen through the disciples on the road to Emmaus. These men were arguing over the events that occurred among them. They had heard the report about the empty tomb and about Jesus being alive, but they doubted Jesus was the promised Savior. Suddenly Jesus appeared on the road, but the men were unable to recognize Him. The risen Savior was before their eyes, but they still could not see the truth. This example tells us there is no correlation between seeing the resurrected Jesus and believing in Him.

With fallen minds, all of us doubt and are unable to believe the truth on our own. Like the disciples, we too are blinded by our sin, so we would likely not have recognized the risen Savior either. But Jesus gives the Holy Spirit whom He called "the Spirit of truth" (John 14:17). The Holy Spirit dwells in us and gifts us with the faith to witness the glory of Jesus and trust in the gospel.

In addition to the Holy Spirit, God has also given the revelation of Jesus Christ in Scripture. On the road to Emmaus, Jesus condemned His disciples for not trusting in God's Word which gave them clear signs to identify the Savior. But Jesus did not leave them in their darkness; He graciously illuminated the Scriptures to them. God's Word, Old Testament to New Testament, is sufficient for us as well. Reading the witness of the Bible today is just as strong as seeing the miracles of Jesus in biblical times (2 Peter 1:16-20). In moments of doubt, we should look to Scripture and pray for the Holy Spirit to help us understand. We can be sure that He will strengthen our weak faith and help us cling to Jesus.

Living with Integrity and Honesty

Believing the truth of the gospel changes how we live. We were dead in sin, rebellious to God's law. We failed to live up to God's command which told us not to bear false witness (Exodus 20:16). As liars, we denied and distorted the truth of God to establish our own way. We lied against ourselves and others in gossip, pretense, cynicism, and empty flattery. But, once we place our faith in Jesus, we are born into a new identity. Jesus perfectly obeyed God's command, and through our faith in Him, we obtain His record. We are clothed in His righteousness and truth. By His Spirit, we undergo an inward transformation into the likeness of Christ. Day by day, our hearts gradually shed their desires to deceive for our own glory. The Holy Spirit gives us the desire to be a truthful people who are obedient to God's words and rightly worship Him.

As the Holy Spirit works in us, we can pursue integrity and honesty with our whole being. In turn, we will experience the fullness of life for which God designed us. Hearts will stand firmly on the Lord and will not be shaken by the world's false promises. Relationships with parents, friends, and church members that were broken because of deceit, mistrust, or secrecy will be restored through vulnerability and faithfulness in Christ. Skeptical, sarcastic, or avoidant thoughts toward others will be made encouraging, loving, and bold. And, our intimacy with God will deepen; we will no longer try to hide from Him, but we will pursue openness with our Creator. Let us love God and our neighbors through being truthful in conversation, on social media, and through our character. A life dedicated to truth is pleasing to God, and it is a sign of gratitude that points others to the saving work of Jesus.

Evangelizing in a *Truthless Culture*

Read Acts 17:22-34

If the historical claims about Jesus are true and if we are truly redeemed by His work, then we must share the gospel. We must speak this truth in a weary world so that others might be saved. We can proclaim the supremacy of Christ over the culture's false beliefs. Every culture tries to grasp for truth but misses the mark apart from Christ. When evangelizing, we can affirm the culture's attempts while confronting the sin.

Ultimately, we want to point them to the more rational, more satisfying, and more liberating message of the gospel. We see an example in Acts 17 when the Apostle Paul confronted pagan worshipers in Athens. Paul was a part of the Jewish religious authority who persecuted Christians. But, after his encounter with the risen Savior, Paul was saved, transformed, and became a leading figure in the spreading of the gospel during the first century A.D.

While in Athens, Paul responded to the idolatrous culture in a Christ-centered way. First, Paul walked around and saw their objects of worship. He affirmed their religiosity as an attempt to understand divine truth and even recited the wisdom of the Athenian poets. Then, Paul confronted their idolatry and called them to repent for rejecting the one true God. He finally pointed them to God's plan of redemption accomplished in Christ. Paul's proof for speaking this way was the historical resurrection of Jesus. Like Paul, we should address the culture's missteps in a gracious yet truthful way. We can refer to the testimony of Scripture and our personal testimonies to verify that the Savior lives and has the utmost authority. Above all, let us pray that the Holy Spirit moves in people's hearts. It is through His power alone that our culture will know the Lord, the Truth who saves.

IN OUR CULTURE, THERE ARE MANY DISTORTIONS OF TRUTH THAT CHALLENGE OUR VIEW OF GOD AND RELIGION. *Having a biblical perspective of truth* CAN HELP US RIGHT THESE DISTORTIONS.

Thank you for studying God's Word with us!

CONNECT WITH US
@thedailygraceco
@dailygracepodcast
@kristinschmucker

CONTACT US
info@thedailygraceco.com

SHARE
#thedailygraceco
#lampandlight

VISIT US ONLINE
www.thedailygraceco.com

MORE DAILY GRACE
The Daily Grace App
Daily Grace Podcast